ADDRESS BOOK

A

Name:	
Address:	

Home No		Cell No	
Work No		Email	

Birthday:	Notes

A

Name:	
Address:	

Home No		Cell No	
Work No		Email	

Birthday:	Notes

A

Name:	
Address:	
Home No	Cell No
Work No	Email
Birthday:	Notes

A

Name:	
Address:	
Home No	Cell No
Work No	Email
Birthday:	Notes

A

Name:	
Address:	

Home No	Cell No
Work No	Email

Birthday:	Notes

A

Name:	
Address:	

Home No	Cell No
Work No	Email

Birthday:	Notes

Name:	
Address:	

Home No	Cell No
Work No	Email

Birthday:	Notes

Name:	
Address:	

Home No	Cell No
Work No	Email

Birthday:	Notes

A

Name:	
Address:	

Home No		Cell No	
Work No		Email	

Birthday:	Notes

A

Name:	
Address:	

Home No		Cell No	
Work No		Email	

Birthday:	Notes

Name:	
Address:	

Home No	Cell No
Work No	Email

Birthday:	Notes

Name:	
Address:	

Home No	Cell No
Work No	Email

Birthday:	Notes

B

Name:	
Address:	

Home No	Cell No
Work No	Email

Birthday:	Notes

B

Name:	
Address:	

Home No	Cell No
Work No	Email

Birthday:	Notes

Name:	
Address:	

Home No	Cell No
Work No	Email

Birthday:	Notes

Name:	
Address:	

Home No	Cell No
Work No	Email

Birthday:	Notes

B

Name:	
Address:	

Home No	Cell No
Work No	Email

Birthday:	Notes

B

Name:	
Address:	

Home No	Cell No
Work No	Email

Birthday:	Notes

Name:	
Address:	

Home No	Cell No
Work No	Email

Birthday:	Notes

Name:	
Address:	

Home No	Cell No
Work No	Email

Birthday:	Notes

B

Name:	
Address:	

Home No	Cell No
Work No	Email

Birthday:	Notes

B

Name:	
Address:	

Home No	Cell No
Work No	Email

Birthday:	Notes

B

Name:	
Address:	

Home No	Cell No
Work No	Email

Birthday:	Notes

B

Name:	
Address:	

Home No	Cell No
Work No	Email

Birthday:	Notes

C

Name:	
Address:	
Home No	Cell No
Work No	Email
Birthday:	Notes

C

Name:	
Address:	
Home No	Cell No
Work No	Email
Birthday:	Notes

Name:	
Address:	

Home No	Cell No
Work No	Email

Birthday:	Notes

Name:	
Address:	

Home No	Cell No
Work No	Email

Birthday:	Notes

C

Name:	
Address:	

Home No	Cell No
Work No	Email

Birthday:	Notes

C

Name:	
Address:	

Home No	Cell No
Work No	Email

Birthday:	Notes

Name:	
Address:	

Home No		Cell No	
Work No		Email	

Birthday:	Notes

Name:	
Address:	

Home No		Cell No	
Work No		Email	

Birthday:	Notes

C

Name:	
Address:	

Home No	Cell No
Work No	Email

Birthday:	Notes

C

Name:	
Address:	

Home No	Cell No
Work No	Email

Birthday:	Notes

Name:	
Address:	

Home No	Cell No
Work No	Email

Birthday:	Notes

Name:	
Address:	

Home No	Cell No
Work No	Email

Birthday:	Notes

D

Name:	
Address:	

Home No	Cell No
Work No	Email

Birthday:	Notes

D

Name:	
Address:	

Home No	Cell No
Work No	Email

Birthday:	Notes

D

Name:	
Address:	

Home No	Cell No
Work No	Email

Birthday:	Notes

D

Name:	
Address:	

Home No	Cell No
Work No	Email

Birthday:	Notes

D

Name:	
Address:	

Home No	Cell No
Work No	Email

Birthday:	Notes

D

Name:	
Address:	

Home No	Cell No
Work No	Email

Birthday:	Notes

D

Name:	
Address:	

Home No	Cell No
Work No	Email

Birthday:	Notes

D

Name:	
Address:	

Home No	Cell No
Work No	Email

Birthday:	Notes

D

Name:	
Address:	

Home No	Cell No
Work No	Email

Birthday:	Notes

D

Name:	
Address:	

Home No	Cell No
Work No	Email

Birthday:	Notes

Name:	
Address:	

Home No	Cell No
Work No	Email

Birthday:	Notes

Name:	
Address:	

Home No	Cell No
Work No	Email

Birthday:	Notes

E

Name:	
Address:	

Home No	Cell No
Work No	Email

Birthday:	Notes

E

Name:	
Address:	

Home No	Cell No
Work No	Email

Birthday:	Notes

E

Name:	
Address:	

Home No	Cell No
Work No	Email

Birthday:	Notes

E

Name:	
Address:	

Home No	Cell No
Work No	Email

Birthday:	Notes

E

Name:	
Address:	

Home No	Cell No
Work No	Email

Birthday:	Notes

E

Name:	
Address:	

Home No	Cell No
Work No	Email

Birthday:	Notes

Name:	
Address:	

Home No		Cell No	
Work No		Email	

Birthday:	Notes

Name:	
Address:	

Home No		Cell No	
Work No		Email	

Birthday:	Notes

E

Name:	
Address:	

Home No		Cell No	
Work No		Email	

Birthday:	Notes

E

Name:	
Address:	

Home No		Cell No	
Work No		Email	

Birthday:	Notes

E

Name:	
Address:	

Home No	Cell No
Work No	Email

Birthday:	Notes

E

Name:	
Address:	

Home No	Cell No
Work No	Email

Birthday:	Notes

F

Name:	
Address:	

Home No	Cell No
Work No	Email

Birthday:	Notes

F

Name:	
Address:	

Home No	Cell No
Work No	Email

Birthday:	Notes

Name:	
Address:	

Home No	Cell No
Work No	Email

Birthday:	Notes

Name:	
Address:	

Home No	Cell No
Work No	Email

Birthday:	Notes

F

Name:	
Address:	

Home No	Cell No
Work No	Email

Birthday:	Notes

F

Name:	
Address:	

Home No	Cell No
Work No	Email

Birthday:	Notes

F

Name:	
Address:	

Home No	Cell No
Work No	Email

Birthday:	Notes

F

Name:	
Address:	

Home No	Cell No
Work No	Email

Birthday:	Notes

F

Name:	
Address:	

Home No	Cell No
Work No	Email

Birthday:	Notes

F

Name:	
Address:	

Home No	Cell No
Work No	Email

Birthday:	Notes

Name:	
Address:	

Home No	Cell No
Work No	Email

Birthday:	Notes

Name:	
Address:	

Home No	Cell No
Work No	Email

Birthday:	Notes

G

Name:	
Address:	

Home No	Cell No
Work No	Email

Birthday:	Notes

G

Name:	
Address:	

Home No	Cell No
Work No	Email

Birthday:	Notes

G

Name:	
Address:	

Home No	Cell No
Work No	Email

Birthday:	Notes

G

Name:	
Address:	

Home No	Cell No
Work No	Email

Birthday:	Notes

G

Name:	
Address:	

Home No	Cell No
Work No	Email

Birthday:	Notes

G

Name:	
Address:	

Home No	Cell No
Work No	Email

Birthday:	Notes

Name:	
Address:	

Home No	Cell No
Work No	Email

Birthday:	Notes

Name:	
Address:	

Home No	Cell No
Work No	Email

Birthday:	Notes

G

Name:	
Address:	

Home No		Cell No	
Work No		Email	

Birthday:	Notes

G

Name:	
Address:	

Home No		Cell No	
Work No		Email	

Birthday:	Notes

Name:	
Address:	
Home No	Cell No
Work No	Email
Birthday:	Notes

Name:	
Address:	
Home No	Cell No
Work No	Email
Birthday:	Notes

H

Name:	
Address:	

Home No	Cell No
Work No	Email

Birthday:	Notes

H

Name:	
Address:	

Home No	Cell No
Work No	Email

Birthday:	Notes

H

Name:	
Address:	

Home No		Cell No	
Work No		Email	

Birthday:	Notes

H

Name:	
Address:	

Home No		Cell No	
Work No		Email	

Birthday:	Notes

Name:	
Address:	
Home No	Cell No
Work No	Email
Birthday:	Notes

Name:	
Address:	
Home No	Cell No
Work No	Email
Birthday:	Notes

Name:	
Address:	

Home No	Cell No
Work No	Email

Birthday:	Notes

Name:	
Address:	

Home No	Cell No
Work No	Email

Birthday:	Notes

Name:	
Address:	

Home No		Cell No	
Work No		Email	

Birthday:	Notes

Name:	
Address:	

Home No		Cell No	
Work No		Email	

Birthday:	Notes

H

Name:	
Address:	

Home No	Cell No
Work No	Email

Birthday:	Notes

H

Name:	
Address:	

Home No	Cell No
Work No	Email

Birthday:	Notes

I

Name:	
Address:	

Home No	Cell No
Work No	Email

Birthday:	Notes

I

Name:	
Address:	

Home No	Cell No
Work No	Email

Birthday:	Notes

Name:	
Address:	
Home No	Cell No
Work No	Email
Birthday:	Notes

Name:	
Address:	
Home No	Cell No
Work No	Email
Birthday:	Notes

/

Name:	
Address:	

Home No		Cell No	
Work No		Email	

Birthday:	Notes

/

Name:	
Address:	

Home No		Cell No	
Work No		Email	

Birthday:	Notes

Name:	
Address:	

Home No	Cell No
Work No	Email

Birthday:	Notes

Name:	
Address:	

Home No	Cell No
Work No	Email

Birthday:	Notes

I

Name:	
Address:	

Home No	Cell No
Work No	Email

Birthday:	Notes

I

Name:	
Address:	

Home No	Cell No
Work No	Email

Birthday:	Notes

Name:	

Address:

Home No	Cell No
Work No	Email

Birthday:	Notes

Name:	

Address:

Home No	Cell No
Work No	Email

Birthday:	Notes

J

Name:	
Address:	

Home No	Cell No
Work No	Email

Birthday:	Notes

J

Name:	
Address:	

Home No	Cell No
Work No	Email

Birthday:	Notes

Name:	
Address:	

Home No	Cell No
Work No	Email

Birthday:	Notes

Name:	
Address:	

Home No	Cell No
Work No	Email

Birthday:	Notes

J

Name:	
Address:	

Home No	Cell No
Work No	Email

Birthday:	Notes

J

Name:	
Address:	

Home No	Cell No
Work No	Email

Birthday:	Notes

J

Name:	
Address:	

Home No	Cell No
Work No	Email

Birthday:	Notes

J

Name:	
Address:	

Home No	Cell No
Work No	Email

Birthday:	Notes

J

Name:	
Address:	

Home No	Cell No
Work No	Email

Birthday:	Notes

J

Name:	
Address:	

Home No	Cell No
Work No	Email

Birthday:	Notes

Name:	
Address:	

Home No	Cell No
Work No	Email

Birthday:	Notes

Name:	
Address:	

Home No	Cell No
Work No	Email

Birthday:	Notes

K

Name:	
Address:	

Home No	Cell No
Work No	Email

Birthday:	Notes

K

Name:	
Address:	

Home No	Cell No
Work No	Email

Birthday:	Notes

K

Name:	
Address:	

Home No	Cell No
Work No	Email

Birthday:	Notes

K

Name:	
Address:	

Home No	Cell No
Work No	Email

Birthday:	Notes

Name:	
Address:	

Home No	Cell No
Work No	Email

Birthday:	Notes

Name:	
Address:	

Home No	Cell No
Work No	Email

Birthday:	Notes

K

Name:	
Address:	
Home No	Cell No
Work No	Email
Birthday:	Notes

K

Name:	
Address:	
Home No	Cell No
Work No	Email
Birthday:	Notes

K

Name:	
Address:	

Home No	Cell No
Work No	Email

Birthday:	Notes

K

Name:	
Address:	

Home No	Cell No
Work No	Email

Birthday:	Notes

K

Name:	
Address:	
Home No	Cell No
Work No	Email
Birthday:	Notes

K

Name:	
Address:	
Home No	Cell No
Work No	Email
Birthday:	Notes

L

Name:	
Address:	

Home No	Cell No
Work No	Email

Birthday:	Notes

L

Name:	
Address:	

Home No	Cell No
Work No	Email

Birthday:	Notes

	L
Name:	
Address:	

Home No	Cell No
Work No	Email

Birthday:	Notes

	L
Name:	
Address:	

Home No	Cell No
Work No	Email

Birthday:	Notes

L

Name:	
Address:	

Home No	Cell No
Work No	Email

Birthday:	Notes

L

Name:	
Address:	

Home No	Cell No
Work No	Email

Birthday:	Notes

L

Name:	
Address:	

Home No	Cell No
Work No	Email

Birthday:	Notes

L

Name:	
Address:	

Home No	Cell No
Work No	Email

Birthday:	Notes

L

Name:	
Address:	

Home No	Cell No
Work No	Email

Birthday:	Notes

L

Name:	
Address:	

Home No	Cell No
Work No	Email

Birthday:	Notes

L

Name:	
Address:	

Home No	Cell No
Work No	Email

Birthday:	Notes

L

Name:	
Address:	

Home No	Cell No
Work No	Email

Birthday:	Notes

M

Name:	
Address:	

Home No	Cell No
Work No	Email

Birthday:	Notes

M

Name:	
Address:	

Home No	Cell No
Work No	Email

Birthday:	Notes

Name:	
Address:	

Home No	Cell No
Work No	Email

Birthday:	Notes

Name:	
Address:	

Home No	Cell No
Work No	Email

Birthday:	Notes

Name:	
Address:	

Home No	Cell No
Work No	Email

Birthday:	Notes

Name:	
Address:	

Home No	Cell No
Work No	Email

Birthday:	Notes

Name:	
Address:	

Home No	Cell No
Work No	Email

Birthday:	Notes

Name:	
Address:	

Home No	Cell No
Work No	Email

Birthday:	Notes

Name:	
Address:	

Home No	Cell No
Work No	Email

Birthday:	Notes

Name:	
Address:	

Home No	Cell No
Work No	Email

Birthday:	Notes

M

Name:	
Address:	

Home No	Cell No
Work No	Email

Birthday:	Notes

M

Name:	
Address:	

Home No	Cell No
Work No	Email

Birthday:	Notes

N

Name:	
Address:	

Home No	Cell No
Work No	Email

Birthday:	Notes

N

Name:	
Address:	

Home No	Cell No
Work No	Email

Birthday:	Notes

Name:	
Address:	

Home No	Cell No
Work No	Email

Birthday:	Notes

Name:	
Address:	

Home No	Cell No
Work No	Email

Birthday:	Notes

N

Name:	
Address:	

Home No	Cell No
Work No	Email

Birthday:	Notes

N

Name:	
Address:	

Home No	Cell No
Work No	Email

Birthday:	Notes

N

Name:	
Address:	

Home No	Cell No
Work No	Email

Birthday:	Notes

N

Name:	
Address:	

Home No	Cell No
Work No	Email

Birthday:	Notes

N

Name:	
Address:	

Home No	Cell No
Work No	Email

Birthday:	Notes

N

Name:	
Address:	

Home No	Cell No
Work No	Email

Birthday:	Notes

Name:	
Address:	

Home No	Cell No
Work No	Email

Birthday:	Notes

Name:	
Address:	

Home No	Cell No
Work No	Email

Birthday:	Notes

O

Name:	
Address:	

Home No	Cell No
Work No	Email

Birthday:	Notes

O

Name:	
Address:	

Home No	Cell No
Work No	Email

Birthday:	Notes

O

Name:	
Address:	

Home No	Cell No
Work No	Email

Birthday:	Notes

O

Name:	
Address:	

Home No	Cell No
Work No	Email

Birthday:	Notes

Name:	
Address:	

Home No	Cell No
Work No	Email

Birthday:	Notes

Name:	
Address:	

Home No	Cell No
Work No	Email

Birthday:	Notes

O

Name:	
Address:	

Home No	Cell No
Work No	Email

Birthday:	Notes

O

Name:	
Address:	

Home No	Cell No
Work No	Email

Birthday:	Notes

O

Name:	
Address:	

Home No	Cell No
Work No	Email

Birthday:	Notes

O

Name:	
Address:	

Home No	Cell No
Work No	Email

Birthday:	Notes

O

Name:	
Address:	

Home No	Cell No
Work No	Email

Birthday:	Notes

O

Name:	
Address:	

Home No	Cell No
Work No	Email

Birthday:	Notes

P

Name:	
Address:	

Home No	Cell No
Work No	Email

Birthday:	Notes

P

Name:	
Address:	

Home No	Cell No
Work No	Email

Birthday:	Notes

Name:	
Address:	
Home No	Cell No
Work No	Email
Birthday:	Notes

Name:	
Address:	
Home No	Cell No
Work No	Email
Birthday:	Notes

P

Name:	
Address:	

Home No	Cell No
Work No	Email

Birthday:	Notes

P

Name:	
Address:	

Home No	Cell No
Work No	Email

Birthday:	Notes

Name:	
Address:	

Home No	Cell No
Work No	Email

Birthday:	Notes

P

Name:	
Address:	

Home No	Cell No
Work No	Email

Birthday:	Notes

P

P

Name:	
Address:	

Home No	Cell No
Work No	Email

Birthday:	Notes

P

Name:	
Address:	

Home No	Cell No
Work No	Email

Birthday:	Notes

Name:	
Address:	
Home No	Cell No
Work No	Email
Birthday:	Notes

Name:	
Address:	
Home No	Cell No
Work No	Email
Birthday:	Notes

Q

Name:	
Address:	

Home No	Cell No
Work No	Email

Birthday:	Notes

Q

Name:	
Address:	

Home No	Cell No
Work No	Email

Birthday:	Notes

Q

Name:	
Address:	
Home No	Cell No
Work No	Email
Birthday:	Notes

Q

Name:	
Address:	
Home No	Cell No
Work No	Email
Birthday:	Notes

Q

Name:	
Address:	

Home No		Cell No	
Work No		Email	

Birthday:	Notes

Q

Name:	
Address:	

Home No		Cell No	
Work No		Email	

Birthday:	Notes

Q

Name:	
Address:	

Home No	Cell No
Work No	Email

Birthday:	Notes

Q

Name:	
Address:	

Home No	Cell No
Work No	Email

Birthday:	Notes

Q

Name:	
Address:	

Home No	Cell No
Work No	Email

Birthday:	Notes

Q

Name:	
Address:	

Home No	Cell No
Work No	Email

Birthday:	Notes

Q

Name:	
Address:	

Home No	Cell No
Work No	Email

Birthday:	Notes

Q

Name:	
Address:	

Home No	Cell No
Work No	Email

Birthday:	Notes

R

Name:	
Address:	

Home No	Cell No
Work No	Email

Birthday:	Notes

R

Name:	
Address:	

Home No	Cell No
Work No	Email

Birthday:	Notes

R

Name:	
Address:	

Home No	Cell No
Work No	Email

Birthday:	Notes

R

Name:	
Address:	

Home No	Cell No
Work No	Email

Birthday:	Notes

R

Name:	
Address:	

Home No		Cell No	
Work No		Email	

Birthday:	Notes

R

Name:	
Address:	

Home No		Cell No	
Work No		Email	

Birthday:	Notes

R

Name:	
Address:	

Home No	Cell No
Work No	Email

Birthday:	Notes

R

Name:	
Address:	

Home No	Cell No
Work No	Email

Birthday:	Notes

R

Name:	
Address:	

Home No	Cell No
Work No	Email

Birthday:	Notes

R

Name:	
Address:	

Home No	Cell No
Work No	Email

Birthday:	Notes

R

Name:	
Address:	

Home No	Cell No
Work No	Email

Birthday:	Notes

R

Name:	
Address:	

Home No	Cell No
Work No	Email

Birthday:	Notes

S

Name:	
Address:	

Home No	Cell No
Work No	Email

Birthday:	Notes

S

Name:	
Address:	

Home No	Cell No
Work No	Email

Birthday:	Notes

S

Name:	
Address:	

Home No	Cell No
Work No	Email

Birthday:	Notes

S

Name:	
Address:	

Home No	Cell No
Work No	Email

Birthday:	Notes

S

Name:	
Address:	

Home No	Cell No
Work No	Email

Birthday:	Notes

S

Name:	
Address:	

Home No	Cell No
Work No	Email

Birthday:	Notes

S

Name:	
Address:	
Home No	Cell No
Work No	Email
Birthday:	Notes

S

Name:	
Address:	
Home No	Cell No
Work No	Email
Birthday:	Notes

S

Name:	
Address:	

Home No	Cell No
Work No	Email

Birthday:	Notes

S

Name:	
Address:	

Home No	Cell No
Work No	Email

Birthday:	Notes

S

Name:	
Address:	

Home No	Cell No
Work No	Email

Birthday:	Notes

S

Name:	
Address:	

Home No	Cell No
Work No	Email

Birthday:	Notes

T

Name:	
Address:	
Home No	Cell No
Work No	Email
Birthday:	Notes

T

Name:	
Address:	
Home No	Cell No
Work No	Email
Birthday:	Notes

	T

Name:	
Address:	

Home No	Cell No
Work No	Email

Birthday:	Notes

	T

Name:	
Address:	

Home No	Cell No
Work No	Email

Birthday:	Notes

T

Name:	

Address:	

Home No	Cell No

Work No	Email

Birthday:	Notes

T

Name:	

Address:	

Home No	Cell No

Work No	Email

Birthday:	Notes

Name:	
Address:	

Home No	Cell No
Work No	Email

Birthday:	Notes

Name:	
Address:	

Home No	Cell No
Work No	Email

Birthday:	Notes

T

Name:	
Address:	

Home No	Cell No
Work No	Email

Birthday:	Notes

T

Name:	
Address:	

Home No	Cell No
Work No	Email

Birthday:	Notes

Name:	
Address:	

Home No	Cell No
Work No	Email

Birthday:	Notes

T

Name:	
Address:	

Home No	Cell No
Work No	Email

Birthday:	Notes

U

Name:	
Address:	

Home No		Cell No	
Work No		Email	

Birthday:	Notes

U

Name:	
Address:	

Home No		Cell No	
Work No		Email	

Birthday:	Notes

Name:	
Address:	

Home No	Cell No
Work No	Email

Birthday:	Notes

Name:	
Address:	

Home No	Cell No
Work No	Email

Birthday:	Notes

U

Name:	
Address:	

Home No	Cell No
Work No	Email

Birthday:	Notes

U

Name:	
Address:	

Home No	Cell No
Work No	Email

Birthday:	Notes

Name:	
Address:	

Home No	Cell No
Work No	Email

Birthday:	Notes

Name:	
Address:	

Home No	Cell No
Work No	Email

Birthday:	Notes

U

Name:	
Address:	

Home No	Cell No
Work No	Email

Birthday:	Notes

U

Name:	
Address:	

Home No	Cell No
Work No	Email

Birthday:	Notes

U

Name:	
Address:	

Home No	Cell No
Work No	Email

Birthday:	Notes

U

Name:	
Address:	

Home No	Cell No
Work No	Email

Birthday:	Notes

V

Name:	
Address:	

Home No	Cell No
Work No	Email

Birthday:	Notes

V

Name:	
Address:	

Home No	Cell No
Work No	Email

Birthday:	Notes

Name:	
Address:	

Home No	Cell No
Work No	Email

Birthday:	Notes

Name:	
Address:	

Home No	Cell No
Work No	Email

Birthday:	Notes

V

Name:	
Address:	

Home No	Cell No
Work No	Email

Birthday:	Notes

V

Name:	
Address:	

Home No	Cell No
Work No	Email

Birthday:	Notes

V

Name:	
Address:	

Home No	Cell No
Work No	Email

Birthday:	Notes

V

Name:	
Address:	

Home No	Cell No
Work No	Email

Birthday:	Notes

V

Name:	
Address:	

Home No	Cell No
Work No	Email

Birthday:	Notes

V

Name:	
Address:	

Home No	Cell No
Work No	Email

Birthday:	Notes

V

Name:	
Address:	

Home No	Cell No
Work No	Email

Birthday:	Notes

V

Name:	
Address:	

Home No	Cell No
Work No	Email

Birthday:	Notes

W

Name:	
Address:	

Home No	Cell No
Work No	Email

Birthday:	Notes

W

Name:	
Address:	

Home No	Cell No
Work No	Email

Birthday:	Notes

W

Name:	
Address:	
Home No	Cell No
Work No	Email
Birthday:	Notes

W

Name:	
Address:	
Home No	Cell No
Work No	Email
Birthday:	Notes

Name:	
Address:	

Home No	Cell No
Work No	Email

Birthday:	Notes

Name:	
Address:	

Home No	Cell No
Work No	Email

Birthday:	Notes

W

Name:	
Address:	
Home No	Cell No
Work No	Email
Birthday:	Notes

W

Name:	
Address:	
Home No	Cell No
Work No	Email
Birthday:	Notes

Name:	
Address:	
Home No	Cell No
Work No	Email
Birthday:	Notes

Name:	
Address:	
Home No	Cell No
Work No	Email
Birthday:	Notes

W

Name:	
Address:	

Home No	Cell No
Work No	Email

Birthday:	Notes

W

Name:	
Address:	

Home No	Cell No
Work No	Email

Birthday:	Notes

| **Name:** | |
| Address: | |

| Home No | Cell No |
| Work No | Email |

| Birthday: | Notes |

| **Name:** | |
| Address: | |

| Home No | Cell No |
| Work No | Email |

| Birthday: | Notes |

X

Name:	
Address:	

Home No	Cell No
Work No	Email

Birthday:	Notes

X

Name:	
Address:	

Home No	Cell No
Work No	Email

Birthday:	Notes

X

Name:	
Address:	

Home No	Cell No
Work No	Email

Birthday:	Notes

X

Name:	
Address:	

Home No	Cell No
Work No	Email

Birthday:	Notes

X

Name:	
Address:	
Home No	Cell No
Work No	Email
Birthday:	Notes

X

Name:	
Address:	
Home No	Cell No
Work No	Email
Birthday:	Notes

Y

Name:	
Address:	

Home No	Cell No
Work No	Email

Birthday:	Notes

Y

Name:	
Address:	

Home No	Cell No
Work No	Email

Birthday:	Notes

Y

Name:	
Address:	
Home No	Cell No
Work No	Email
Birthday:	Notes

Y

Name:	
Address:	
Home No	Cell No
Work No	Email
Birthday:	Notes

Y

Name:	
Address:	

Home No	Cell No
Work No	Email

Birthday:	Notes

Y

Name:	
Address:	

Home No	Cell No
Work No	Email

Birthday:	Notes

Y

Name:	
Address:	

Home No	Cell No
Work No	Email

Birthday:	Notes

Y

Name:	
Address:	

Home No	Cell No
Work No	Email

Birthday:	Notes

Y

Name:	
Address:	

Home No	Cell No
Work No	Email

Birthday:	Notes

Y

Name:	
Address:	

Home No	Cell No
Work No	Email

Birthday:	Notes

Name:	
Address:	

Home No	Cell No
Work No	Email

Birthday:	Notes

Name:	
Address:	

Home No	Cell No
Work No	Email

Birthday:	Notes

Z

Name:	
Address:	

Home No	Cell No
Work No	Email

Birthday:	Notes

Z

Name:	
Address:	

Home No	Cell No
Work No	Email

Birthday:	Notes

Z

Name:	
Address:	
Home No	Cell No
Work No	Email
Birthday:	Notes

Z

Name:	
Address:	
Home No	Cell No
Work No	Email
Birthday:	Notes

Z

Name:	
Address:	

Home No	Cell No
Work No	Email

Birthday:	Notes

Z

Name:	
Address:	

Home No	Cell No
Work No	Email

Birthday:	Notes

Z

Name:	
Address:	

Home No	Cell No
Work No	Email

Birthday:	Notes

Z

Name:	
Address:	

Home No	Cell No
Work No	Email

Birthday:	Notes

Z

Name:	
Address:	

Home No	Cell No
Work No	Email

Birthday:	Notes

Z

Name:	
Address:	

Home No	Cell No
Work No	Email

Birthday:	Notes

Name:	
Address:	
Home No	Cell No
Work No	Email
Birthday:	Notes

Name:	
Address:	
Home No	Cell No
Work No	Email
Birthday:	Notes

Made in United States
Orlando, FL
20 June 2025

62275129R00089